MW00570274

ELEMENTS OF YOGA

Sri Aurobindo

ELEMENTS OF YOGA

SRI AUROBINDO ASHRAM
PONDICHERRY

First edition 1953
Second edition 2001
Fourth impression 2012

Rs 40
ISBN 978-81-7058-660-9

Published by Sri Aurobindo Ashram Publication Department
Pondicherry 605 002
Web http://www.sabda.in

Printed at Sri Aurobindo Ashram Press, Pondicherry
PRINTED IN INDIA

Publisher's Note

This book is a compilation of Sri Aurobindo's replies to elementary questions about Yoga raised by a disciple during the years 1933 to 1936. It was first published in 1953 and reissued in 1956. In 1991 the text was reproduced as the first part of *Commentaries on "Elements of Yoga"* by the Mother. *Elements of Yoga* is now being issued independently again in a second edition.

Contents

1. *The Call and Fitness*

How can one know if he is fit for the spiritual life before taking up Yoga?

How can anyone know before he puts his step on the path? He can only know whether he has the aspiration or not, whether he feels a call or not.

*

You have said that to enter the path of Yoga "all one needs to know is whether the soul in one has been moved to the Yoga or not". But how to know this clearly before entering the path?

It is a question of feeling it or not. There is no "how to know" about it. One knows or one does not know, one feels or one does not feel. You don't ask how to know when one is happy or angry or sorrowful — one knows at once.

*

How can people know whether they have any spiritual possibility in them?

Nobody does know. When the soul pushes them, they turn towards the Divine, that is all.

*

Please let me know if I have any possibility for spiritual realisation.

It is a waste of time to ask such a question. When you have entered the spiritual path, you have only to go on relying not on your possibility but on the Mother's Power.

*

Is it not true that those who enter the path of Yoga without the full knowledge of their nature and its possibilities get into difficulties?

Who comes into the path of Yoga with full knowledge or any knowledge? All are ignorant; it is only by Yoga itself that they get the knowledge.

*

Sometimes a person enters the path because he feels the aspiration and the call but afterwards leaves it. What is the reason? Is it not because before entering it he was not able to judge the possibility of his nature?

Because his aspiration flags or because he is unfaithful to the call. It is not a question of judging. I have told you nobody can know or judge.

*

Some people say that unless the whole nature is purified there can be no real beginning of Yoga. Is this true?

It is absurd to say that.

*

Is it true that only a person who has some experiences and realisations in sadhana is accepted by the Mother while one who has no such experiences and lives in ordinary consciousness is not accepted by her?

Why should he not be accepted by the Mother? What do you mean by "accepted"?

*

If a sadhak cannot open himself fully to the Mother because of the obstacles in his nature, will he not be accepted by the Mother?

There is no meaning in such a question. Those who follow the Yoga here are accepted by the Mother — for "accepted" means "admitted into the Yoga, accepted as disciples". But the progress in the Yoga and the Siddhi in the Yoga depend on the degree to which there is the opening.

*

When a sadhak is faced with serious difficulties in his sadhana over and over again and is not able to reject his lower nature, what will help him to keep up his faith and stick to the path?

Who is able to reject the lower nature fully? All one can do is to aspire and reject the lower impulses and call in the Divine to do the rest.

*

It is said in the Gita that out of thousands only a few seek the Divine and even of these few only one or two can reach Him. Is this true?

If one goes by one's own strength, very few can do it — but by faith in the Divine, by the Grace of the Divine, it becomes possible.

*

What should be the final aim of a sadhak? Should it not be to become a Yogi?

To be in full union with the Divine is the final aim. When one has some kind of constant union, one can be called a Yogi, but the union has to be made complete. There are Yogis who have only the union on the spiritual plane, others who are united in mind and heart, others in the vital also. In our Yoga our aim is to be united too in the physical consciousness and on the supramental plane.

2. *The Foundation*

When can it be said that a sadhak has laid his foundation in sadhana?

When he has a settled calm and equality and devotion and a continuity of spiritual experience.

*

What is the right way to establish peace and equality in the nature?

The peace and the equality are there above you, you have to call them down into the mind and vital and the body. And whenever something disturbs, you have to reject the thing that disturbs and the disturbance.

*

Do calm and equality come down from above by the Mother's Grace?

When they descend, it is by the soul's aspiration and the Mother's Grace.

*

What is the true sign indicating that equality is established in the nature? Is it to receive all the disturbance from outside or inside in perfect calm and without doing anything to remedy it?

It is to face it without being disturbed and to reject it calmly. Whether one tries to remedy or not remedy should make no difference. Only when one acts against it, one must do it calmly, without anger, excitement, grief or any other disturbing movement.

*

When a person has attained samatā or equality, can we say that he is egoless?

Samata does not mean the absence of ego, but the absence of desire and attachment. The ego-sense may disappear or it may remain in a subtilised or dense form — it depends on the person.

*

Does the Divine descent mean descent of Peace, Purity and Silence?

It is part of the Divine descent, not the whole of it.

*

I find that when Peace has come down in my being there is a play of a higher Force in it. Is this Force different from the force of Peace?

The peace is the condition of the right play of the Force. Force and Peace are two different powers of the Divine.

*

How to develop the capacity to receive the Divine Force?

Quietness of mind is the first requisite — for the rest aspiration and *abhyās*.

*

What is the exact meaning of calm mind? Does it mean that there will be no thought at all in the mind?

No. It is not necessary that there should be no thought. When there is no thought, it is silence. But the mind is said to be calm when thoughts, feelings, etc., may pass through it, but it is not disturbed. It feels that the thoughts are not its own; it observes them perhaps; but it is not perturbed by anything.

*

What is the real meaning of activity and passivity in sadhana?

Activity in aspiration, Tapasya, rejection of the wrong forces ; passivity to the true working, the working of the Mother's Force, are the right things in sadhana.

3. *Aspiration*

What is meant by spiritual aspiration?

It means the aspiration towards spiritual things, spiritual experience, spiritual realisation, the Divine.

*

Are will and aspiration the same?

No, certainly not. Aspiration is a call to the Divine, — will is the pressure of a conscious force on Nature.

*

Is prayer the same as aspiration?

It is an expression of aspiration or can be. For there are prayers which only express a desire — e.g., prayers for wealth, worldly success, etc.

*

What is the difference between aspiration and opening?

They have nothing to do with each other, except that aspiration brings opening. Opening means that the consciousness becomes opened to the Truth or the Divine to which it is now shut — it indicates a state of receptivity.

Aspiration is a call in the being, it is not opening.

*

Is the aspiration rising from the vital of the same nature as that rising from the heart?

No, the vital is dynamic, a call from the Life-force — that from the heart is either emotional or psychic.

*

Does the power of aspiration vary in different sadhaks according to their natures?

No. Aspiration is the same power in all; it differs only in purity, intensity and object.

*

Can a person with a weak will progress in sadhana by aspiration only?

No. He must either increase his will-power or call in a Higher Power to do it for him.

*

Can aspiration increase the will-power of a person whose will is weak?

Yes, it can — by calling in the Divine Will.

*

Why does aspiration become sometimes slow and sometimes rapid?

It is so with everyone — the nature cannot always go at a rapid pace.

*

If the nature connot always go at a rapid pace, why are we asked to remain constant in aspiration?

If you are not constant in aspiration, the nature will then sink back into the old lower ways.

*

Will a sadhak who feels neither any intense aspiration nor any acute resistance of the obstacles of his nature, be able to go forward in his sadhana?

I suppose it means that he can only progress slowly.

*

When a sadhak does not feel any aspiration and does not get any experience, what should he do to stick on to his sadhana?

Remember the Mother, remain quiet and call.

*

Is it possible for a sadhak to realise the Divine fully from the beginning by the power of his aspiration?

If there is the full purity of the psychic and spiritual aspiration, then that can happen — but it is rare.

*

I feel that aspiration also is increased by the Mother's Will and Grace. Is it not so?

Yes, but not if you do not aspire.

*

You have asked me to have ceaseless aspiration. But I find that it is the Mother's Force that kindles up aspiration and strengthens and increases it in me. What personal effort on my part is then needed?

It is true that it is the Mother's Force that aspires in you, but if the personal consciousness does not give its assent, then the Force does not work. If the personal consciousnes ceaselessly looks for the Divine and assents to the working, the aspiration and the working of the Force become also ceaseless.

*

But is it not true that the personal consciousness of the sadhak is also moved by the Mother and all his actions governed by her?

But if your personal consciousness does wrong things, it is also the Mother who does those wrong things?

*

But is it not a fact that if a sadhak is not open to the Mother's working in his higher parts, the Mother works in his lower parts and makes him commit mistakes so that he may learn through the suffering brought by them to turn to her in his higher parts?

The Mother does not make people commit mistakes; it is the Prakriti that makes them do it — if the Purusha does not refuse his consent. The Mother here is not this lower Prakriti, but the Divine Shakti and it is her work to press on this lower Nature to change. You can say that under the pressure, the Prakriti stumbles and is unable to reply perfectly and makes mistakes. But it is not the Mother who makes you do wrong movements or does the wrong movements in you — if you think that, you are in danger of justifying the movements or their continuance.

*

But is it not a fact that Prakriti herself comes from the Divine? In that case is she not a power and a portion of the Divine Mother?

Everything comes from the Divine; but the lower Prakriti is the power of the Ignorance — it is not therefore a power of truth, but only of mixed truth and falsehood. The Mother here stands not for the Power of Ignorance, but for the Power that has come down to bring down the Truth and raise up to the Truth out of the Ignorance.

*

In what way my personal effort is needed to assent to the Mother's working in me?

By opening yourself more and more by assent to the true things, Peace, Light, Truth, Ananda — by refusing the wrong things, such as anger, falsehood, lust, etc.

*

What are the obstacles in the way of giving full assent to the Mother's working in the sadhak's nature?

It is the wrong movements, — self-will, egoism, the vital passions, vanity, personal desire, etc.

*

Is it true that if a person has true aspiration, the Divine makes him a fit receptacle for His descent in him even if his mind is ignorant and limited?

Yes — only the mind must not be small and narrow — and in love with its narrowness.

*

What is meant by being in love with the mind's narrowness?

People like to be narrow; they are attached to their own limited ideas, feelings, opinions, preferences and get disturbed, angry or full of doubt if anyone tries to make them think more widely — that is being in love with the mind's narrowness.

*

Some people say that a scholarly person with a developed intellect progresses in sadhana more rapidly than an uneducated person with an undeveloped intellect even though both have the same intensity of aspiration, Is this true?

There is no such rule. It is better if the mind is strong and developed, but scholarship does not necessarily create a strong and developed mind.

*

You say that scholarship does not create a strong and developed mind. What creates it then?

It creates itself by the will to know rightly, widely and with a plastic reception of the truth.

*

Is it necessary for a person with a weak and narrow mind to make effort to make his mind strong and developed in order to receive the Divine Grace or he can leave it to the Grace itself to prepare it for its descent?

It depends on the person. If his weak or narrow mind is coming in the way of his sadhana, he can make the attempt to broaden it — if the heart is strong and true or the psychic being active, then he can leave it to the Divine Force to do it in the course of the Yoga.

*

For the proper education and cultural development of the mind is reading of books not necessary for a sadhak?

It is not by reading books that he can do it — it is by trying to think and see things clearly that it comes. Reading is a quite secondary thing. One may read thousands of books, yet remain narrow and foolish.

*

Is it true that "satsanga" (company of spiritual persons) creates and increases the aspiration for the Divine?

Yes.

4. Sincerity

*Is it true that it is only through the power of abso-
lute sincerity that one can get full transformation and
reach the Supramental Truth?*

Yes.

*

*The Mother has said: "If you are not sincere do not
begin Yoga." Does this imply that if after entering
Yoga a person finds that his sincerity is not complete, he should leave it?*

No. It is only if he is fundamentally insincere that he
should leave it.

*

*How can a sadhak know whether he is fundamen-
tally insincere?*

If he sees that he is full of ego and doing sadhana for the
sake of the ego only and has no real turning towards the
Divine.

*

*Is there no possibility for a sadhak to get rid of his
fundamental insincerity?*

If the sadhak becomes aware of his insincerity and sincerely wants to get rid of it, he can.

*

How can a sadhak know whether he is growing in sincerity?

By seeing whether he responds to the Divine forces only or still responds to, accepts and harbours the ego-forces and desire-forces.

*

Is it true that if a sadhak has complete sincerity he can make rapid progress even if his devotion is deficient?

If he is sincere, there is bound to be devotion. Sincerity in Yoga means to respond to the Divine alone and if he has no devotion he cannot do it.

*

What is the right attitude to stick on to this path till the Supramental Truth is realised?

There is the psychic condition and sincerity and devotion to the Mother.

*

Is it a sign of sincerity to confess one's weaknesses and faults to the Divine and to others?

Why to others? One has to confess them to the Divine.

*

But if one does some wrong to a person, is it not necessary to confess it to him? Is it enough to confess it to the Divine?

If it concerns the other persons, then it can be done.

*

How can the sadhaks avoid being misled by the forces of falsehood in their sadhana?

They have to be always sincere — it depends upon that.

*

How long is it necessary for the sadhaks to live in discipline?

Till they get the realisation at least.

*

Does this mean that they have to live in discipline till they get the complete realisation?

At any rate a fundamental realisation so that they will no longer seek to act according to their mental fancy or vital ego.

*

What is meant by "fundamental realisation"? Does it refer to the condition of those sadhaks who are fully surrendered to the Divine and completely transformed?

That is the complete realisation. If they are fully transformed, there is no more sadhana.

*

What is meant by "mental fancy"?

When the mind follows its own ideas for the pleasure of it and out of attachment to them, not caring for the Truth.

*

Is it possible for the sadhaks who have not got rid of mental fancy and vital ego to get even a partial realisation?

No, they must be surrendered to the Divine.

*

Is it sufficient to get rid of mental fancy and vital ego to reach the fundamental realisation?

No. He must surrender and his psychic must be in front and dominate the mind and vital.

5. *Faith*

What is the difference between faith, belief and confidence?

Faith is a feeling in the whole being; belief is mental; confidence means trust in a person or in the Divine or a feeling of surety about the result of one's seeking or endeavour.

*

What do people mean by "blind faith"?

The phrase has no real meaning. I suppose they mean they will not believe without proof — but the conclusion formed after proof is not faith, it is knowledge or it is a mental opinion. Faith is something which one has before proof or knowledge and it helps you to arrive at knowledge or experience. There is no proof that God exists, but if I have faith in God, then I can arrive at the experience of the Divine.

*

What is the difference between psychic faith, mental faith, vital faith and physical faith?

Mental faith combats doubt and helps to open to the true knowledge; vital faith prevents the attacks of the hostile forces or defeats them and helps to open to the true spiritual will and action; physical faith keeps one firm through all physical obscurity, inertia or suffering and helps to open to the foundation of the true consciousness; psychic faith opens to the direct touch of the Divine and helps to bring union and surrender.

*

What is meant by "dynamic faith"? Is not all faith dynamic?

Faith can be Tamasic and ineffective, e.g. "I believe the Mother will do everything, so I will do nothing. When she wants, she will transform me." That is not a dynamic but a static and inert faith.

*

Even after the sadhaks have complete faith and surrender, have they to wait long to get the higher experiences by the Divine Grace ?

If the faith and surrender are complete in every part, it is not possible that there should be no experience.

6. *Surrender*

Is it not possible to transform the being without sur-render?

If there is no surrender, there can be no transformation of the whole being.

*

When does real surrender begin in a sadhak?

It begins when there is the true self-offering.

*

How to bring about true self-offering?

By not following ego and desire. It is ego and desire that prevent surrender.

*

What is the sign to indicate that a sadhak's determi-nation to surrender to the Divine is having practical effect in his life?

The sign is that he has full obedience without question or revolt or demand or condition and that he answers to all divine influences and rejects all that are not from the Divine.

*

Is it not a fact that even after repeated determination to surrender the old habits come in the way of its effective realisation?

Yes, certainly — they always do that till the sincerity and purity and surrender are complete.

✻

What is the most powerful way to make the determination of surrender rapidly effective?

Absolute sincerity.

✻

When does the Divine himself fully take up the sadhana and carry it out for the sadhaks?

When they give up the ego.

✻

What is meant by the Divine taking up the sadhana?

When it is the Divine Force that works out all the Yoga and the actions by a direct action of which the sadhak is conscious.

✻

How can one know that one's sadhana has been taken up by the Divine?

You can feel it.

✻

The Gita's central secret is to surrender to the Divine by rejecting all dharmas, "sarva dharmān parityajya". What is the meaning of "sarva dharmān"?

All formations based on the mind's preferences, the vital's desires, the physical's attachments to its habits.

*

Is it possible for a sadhak to reject all dharmas from the beginning of his sadhana?

No, it takes time — but the will to surrender must be there.

*

For offering all movements of the nature to the Divine, it is first necessary to observe them. How to make this power of observation true and complete?

By looking and observing vigilantly and letting nothing escape one's observation of oneself and by aspiring for still greater power of vision until it is complete.

*

What is the difference between active and passive surrender?

Active surrender is when you associate your will with the Divine Will, reject what is not the Divine, assent to what is the Divine. Passive surrender is when everything is left entirely to the Divine — that few can really do, because in practice it turns out that you surrender to the lower nature under pretext of surrendering to the Divine.

*

What is meant by "Detailed surrender" — the flower which the Mother sometimes gives?

Surrender in every action and every detail of one's nature.

*

Is it true that until a sadhak's sincerity and surrender are complete, he has to undergo many sufferings?

He need not suffer if he takes the true way, but he has to deal with the difficulties.

*

In "Conversations", the Mother says that if the central being is surrendered then the chief difficulty is gone. What is this central being ? Is it the psychic?

The central being is the Purusha. If it is surrendered, then all the other beings can be offered to the Divine and the psychic being brought in front.

*

What is the function of this Purusha which you say is the central being and where is it located?

Purusha is the conscious being who supports all the action of Nature. There is no fixed place, but as the central being he usually stands above the *ādhār* — he becomes also the mental, vital, physical, psychic being.

*

Is the Purusha the soul in man?

No, the psychic being is the soul in man.

*

How long does the Purusha take to surrender completely to the Divine?

There is no fixed time.

*

How can one swiftly surrender the Purusha to the Divine?

By aspiration and by Divine Grace.

*

Is it the Purusha who consents to the action of the Mother's Force and Grace in the being?

Yes.

*

Are all the beings (mental, vital, physical and psychic) under the influence of the Purusha?

He presides in a way over all.

*

If the Purusha does not consent to the action of the Mother's Grace, does it prevent the other beings from receiving or feeling the Mother's Grace for transformation?

No. The Purusha often holds back and lets the other beings consent or feel in his place.

*

When a sadhak feels the Mother's Grace coming down in him, is it due to the Mother's consent?

What do you mean by consent? The Mother's Grace comes down by the Mother's will. The Purusha can accept or reject the Grace.

7. *Love*

Can psychic love reach the Highest Truth by its own power?

Yes, certainly.

*

How can one know that he has full psychic love for the Divine?

By the absence of ego, by pure devotion, by submission and surrender to the Divine.

*

Is psychic love always turned towards the Divine?

It is sometimes turned to the human person, but it never gets its true satisfaction till it turns to the Divine.

*

Is not psychic love the same as divine Love?

No. There is a human psychic love also marked by self-lessness, fidelity and self-giving to a human being.

*

Can human love if it takes a psychic turn not lead to divine Love?

One can pass from one to the other.

*

Can divine Love not be expressed through human emotions?

How can divine Love be expressed through human emotions ? It becomes then human, not divine. If you mean there is something corresponding but much greater in divine Love, that may be.

*

Can one not realise spiritual truth through psychicised human love?

No — one only gets faint glimpses of something, one does not realise.

*

Is it not that the motive which leads people to begin Yoga is divine Love?

No — there may be a human love turning towards the Divine. But Yoga begins from many motives, not love alone.

*

Is there no emotion in the divine Love?

There is an intense feeling — there is not what men call

emotion, — for that is superficial and transient. The intensity of divine Love never creates a disturbance anywhere in the being.

*

Is emotion an expression of Ananda?

How does emotion express Ananda? Emotion may be one result of a touch of Ananda in the consciousness, but it does not express Ananda. Ananda is itself its own expression.

*

What is the true way to manifest divine Love?

By a more and more selfless turning to the Divine.

*

Is it possible to receive Divine Love before full transformation?

Partly.

*

Is love the only power of the psychic or there are other powers in it?

In the psychic there are plenty of powers — faith, psychic sight, gratitude to the Divine, fire of aspiration and many others.

*

Is there any "abhimān" in psychic love?

None. *Abhimān* is sheer egoism.

*

Is not ordinary human love a shadow of psychic love?

No, certainly not. Ordinary human love is vital, emotional and physical and always egoistic — a form of self-
love. The psychic element is very small except in a few.

*

*Can there be any manifestation of psychic love in
the physical?*

There can be — it must have no taint of sexuality in it.

*

Is there any psychic love in animals?

Their sexual love is vital-physical — the rest also mostly.
Some psychic element does come in the higher kinds.
Some animals have a psychic affection for men.

*

*How to distinguish between psychic bhakti, mental
bhakti and vital bhakti for the Mother?*

The psychic is made up of love and self-giving without
demand, the vital of the will to be possessed by the Mother

and serve her, the mental of faith and unquestioning acceptance of all that the Mother is, says and does. These, however, are outside signs — it is in inner character quite recognizable but not to be put into words that they differ.

*

Is there no use of mental and vital bhakti in our Yoga?

Who says there is not? So long as it is real devotion, all Bhakti has a place.

*

Is psychic bhakti the same as perfect devotion?

It is the basis of perfect devotion.

*

What is the difference between psychic emotion and psychic bhakti?

Bhakti is psychic emotion, psychic feeling directed towards the Divine, the Guru, etc.

*

What is the meaning of "Prem Bhakti"? In what way is it different from simple bhakti?

I suppose it is Bhakti with love as its basis; there can be Bhakti of worship, submission, reverence, obedience, etc., but without love.

*

I often feel an aspiration to see all in the Mother and the Mother in all. Will it be fulfilled?

To see all in the Mother and the Mother in all is a necessary experience in the Yoga. There is no reason why it should not happen.

*

Often a very strong feeling comes to me that I am very far from the Mother. Why do I have this feeling?

It is the feeling of the physical or outward being which is by its ignorance unable to feel the Mother's nearness.

*

How to overcome this feeling of being far away from the Mother?

The Mother is always near and within, it is only the obscurity of mind and vital that does not see or feel it. That is a knowledge which the mind ought to hold firmly.

*

What is the right way of maintaining a relation of harmony and good will with others?

In the life of Yoga it is the psychic alone that can do that. The mind and vital can only do it with this or that person with whom it has a mental or vital affinity and it is not the real thing.

*

If my love is associated with demand, is it vital love?

Yes, that is the nature of vital love. It is based on desire and the sense of claim or sense of possession; psychic love is based on self-giving.

*

"If you love me, I will love you"; is this not an expression of vital love?

Yes — bargaining vital love.

*

"Even if you hate me and do not care for me, I will love you"; can this be an expression of vital love?

It may be the expression of a certain kind of passionate vital love — but it can also be the expression of a certain kind of psychic love too.

*

"I will love you as much as you love me"; what kind of love is revealed in this expression?

It is not love at all — it is commercial barter.

8. The Psychic Opening

In "Conversations", the Mother speaks of a fire burning in the deep quietude of the heart. Is this fire the psychic being?

A fire is not a being — it is the psychic fire, an intense condition of aspiration.

*

Where is the psychic being located?

It is behind the heart centre, deep in.

*

The Mother sometimes says that the psychic being of this or that person is good. But is it not a fact that the psychic being in all is a portion of the Divine and therefore always good? Why then does Mother make a distinction in particular cases?

The psychic being develops — in some it is strong enough to overcome easily the mental and vital resistance — in some it is less developed and has more difficulty.

*

Does not the power of Yoga come first through the psychic and then produce a swift change in the mind?

Not necessarily. Most people begin with the power working in the mind — it is only when the mind and vital have been changed to some extent before that the psychic is ready to come forward.

*

Can the psychic being manifest itself directly without the help of mental, vital and physical beings?

The mind, life and body are the instruments for manifestation. Of course, the psychic can manifest things by itself inwardly or in its own plane, but for manifestation in the physical plane the instrumentality of other parts is needed.

*

Is it not possible to bring the psychic being forward without changing the mind and vital?

No. If they are unchanged they prevent the psychic from coming forward.

*

What is the difference between the spiritual and psychic consciousness?

The Spirit is the consciousness above mind, the Atman or Self, which is always in oneness with the Divine — a spiritual consciousness is one which is always in unity or at least in contact with the Divine.

The psychic is a spark come from the Divine which is there in all things and as the individual evolves it grows in him and manifests as the psychic being, the soul, seeking always for the Divine and the Truth and answering to the Divine and the Truth whenever and wherever it meets it.

*

What is the difference between the Divine and the Spirit?

The Divine is everywhere even in the Ignorance. It is not only the Spirit, but it is in mind, life and body. What stands behind mind, life and body is the Spirit.

*

Are there many psychic planes?

No, there is only one.

*

Can a person whose psychic being is not sufficiently developed, overcome the fundamental difficulties of his nature?

No, not by his own strength; but with the Divine Grace supporting him he can.

*

Is it true that if the psychic being comes to the front

all doubts and difficulties can be swiftly destroyed?

Yes.

*

How to bring the psychic being in front? Can it be done by avoiding wrong movements?

That is the negative way; the positive way is obedience to the Divine, devotion, surrender.

*

Can the psychic being be brought and kept always in front by making the physical consciousness plastic?

No, that is rather a result of the spiritual and psychic development acting on the body consciousness.

*

Nowadays I feel very intensely a sorrow which brings a flow of tears in my eyes. There is no unrest or disturbance in it, rather there is a feeling of calm and purity and a deep gravity associated with it. Is this what is called the psychic sorrow?

Yes, there is a psychic sorrow of that kind — but psychic tears need not be sorrowful, there are also tears of emotion and joy.

9. *Experiences and Visions*

What is the difference between concentration and meditation in our Yoga?

Concentration, for our Yoga, means when the consciousness is fixed in a particular state (e.g., peace) or movement (e.g., aspiration, will, coming into contact with the Mother, taking the Mother's name); meditation is when the inner mind is looking at things to get the right knowledge.

*

You wrote that "the Mother is always in concentrated consciousness in her inner being". What is meant by "concentrated consciousness"?

The higher consciousness is a concentrated consciousness, concentrated in the Divine Unity and in the working out of the Divine Will, not dispersed and rushing about after this or that mental idea or vital desire or physical need as is the ordinary human consciousness — also not invaded by a hundred haphazard thoughts, feelings and impulses, but master of itself, centred and harmonious.

*

What is the sign of successful meditation?

To enter into a deeper or higher consciousness or for that deeper or higher consciousness to descend into you — that is true success of meditation.

*

Is it true that without meditation it is impossible to get higher experiences?

It is easier with some meditation — but people do get these things who never sit in meditation — so what is the use of saying "impossible"?

*

Does sitting in an asana have any effect on meditation?

The effect is to strengthen the vital forces, especially to consolidate them in the body.

*

Do all sadhaks have similar kinds of experiences and realisations in the development of their sadhana or these things vary according to their nature?

There is something common to all — all the essential things are in possibility common to all, but each develops what he can, in the way he can, according to his nature.

*

What is the difference between experience, realisation and siddhi?

Experience is a word that covers almost all the happenings in Yoga; only when something gets settled, then it is no longer an experience but part of the Siddhi; e.g., peace when it comes and goes is an experience — when it is settled and goes no more it is Siddhi. Realisation is different — it is when something for which you are aspiring becomes real to you; e.g., you have the idea of the Divine in all, but it is only an idea, a belief; when you feel or see the Divine in all, it becomes a realisation.

*

What is the difference between vision, experience and realisation?

When you see Light, that is vision; when you feel Light entering into you, that is experience; when Light settles in you and brings illumination and knowledge, that is a realisation. But ordinarily visions are also called experiences.

*

What is the difference between feeling and realisation?

One can realise the Divine by feeling the Divine or by seeing or by both.

*

What is the difference between the visions of the vital plane and those of the spiritual plane?

Visions do not come from the spiritual plane — they come from the subtle physical, the vital, the mental, the psychic or from the planes above the Mind. What comes from the spiritual plane are experiences of the Divine, e.g., the experience of self everywhere, of the Divine in all, etc.

*

Is it possible to get the higher experience before the nature is transformed?

Yes, but then it does not transform the nature, it is only an experience of the inner consciousness in its own field and even there no real perfection is possible.

*

There are people who frequently have dreams and visions of the vital plane. Is it an indication of their high spiritual development?

No. They are helpful for developing beyond the ordinary limited physical consciousness and becoming aware of things behind and the forces that move the being. Unless one knows the things of the mental and vital plane, one cannot have a complete self-knowledge.

*

Is it possible to have spiritual development without seeing anything psychically?

What do you mean by seeing "psychically"? Is it visions or the psychic sight of the Truth, psychic perception? One develops by spiritual knowledge and experience which comes from above the mind or one develops by psychic perception and experience which comes from within — these are the two main things. But it is also necessary to grow by inner mental and vital experiences, and visions and dream-experiences play a large part here. One thing may predominate in one sadhak, others in another; each develops according to his nature.

*

Is there any difference between experience and knowledge?

When you have a symbolic dream, that is an experience; when you know what it means, that is knowledge.

*

When will I get clear knowledge to understand and interpret my visions and experiences?

When by practice and intuition you begin to learn what things mean in the different planes. You have to grow more conscious and observant, that is all.

10. *Work*

When people join the Ashram to do sadhana and live under the Mother's protection, is it not necessary for them to do some Ashram work to progress in their sadhana?

They should do.

*

Should they ask the Mother for work or wait till she herself gives them work?

If they have the true spirit in them, they will ask for work.

*

Sometimes when a sadhak asks the Mother's permission to do a work of his choice and the Mother gives it, can it be said that it is the work done for the Mother?

The sadhak ought to be ready to do any work that is needed, not only the work he prefers.

*

Some say that if a sadhak asks Mother's permission for a work and she gives it, it cannot be said to be directly the Mother's work. Only the work given by the Mother herself is her work. Is this true?

It depends on the circumstances.

*

I find that when something is required to be done in the Ashram the sadhaks usually say: "I will do it, if the Mother asks me." Often necessary work is thus neglected in the Mother's name.

If they sincerely depend upon the Mother's directions, it is all right; if it is a mere excuse for not doing something that ought to be done, it is another matter. But it depends upon the case — the discrimination of one man is not the same as that of another nor the commonsense either. One may think a thing right to do, another may not see it in the same way.

*

Sometimes when help is urgently required in some work and a sadhak is approached to render it, he says: "I cannot give even a minute's help without the Mother's order." Does he say this out of sincere understanding?

Usually he is not sincere — it means that he does not want to do it.

*

Some people in the Ashram say: "If the Mother herself does not give us any work to do, why should we ask her to give us work? If it is her wish she will

*herself give us work, there is no need for us to ask."
How far are these people right in their understanding?*

There is no reason why one should not offer to work if
there is work to do. Often there is work to be done and
no one offers, so it is not done. Most of the Ashram work
is done by a few people, while others do a little only or
only what they please.

*

*What is meant by your writing that "most of the
Ashram work is done by a few people while others
do a little only or do what they please"? Is it meant
that these others work only for their satisfaction and
convenience and not for the Mother's?*

I simply noted the fact that the zealous workers are few
and whenever a work has to be done it is they who come
forward — the rest do without enthusiasm some fixed
work chosen by themselves or else do nothing or practi-
cally nothing at all.

*

*If a sadhak finds himself incapable of doing medita-
tion, can he progress in sadhana by only doing work
for the Mother?*

If he does the work in a consecrated spirit opening to the
Mother and to her consciousness and force.

*

If a person joins the Ashram and does the work given by the Mother sincerely but finds that he often gets into a bad condition, is he really not a sadhak? Does it mean that he is not doing the work in the true spirit of consecration?

It depends on the sadhak. None keep the good condition at all times, that is not the point. If he is fundamentally sincere in the work and the sadhana, he is a sadhak; but if he works merely because he has to work or if he works in a selfish spirit, then it cannot be called a spirit of consecration.

*

Some people say that many persons who do not understand anything about Yoga are taken as permanent sadhaks by the Mother and given some work only to give them a chance to come into the possibility of Yoga. What is the truth in this?

What you report them as saying seems to be without meaning.

*

My faith is that Sri Aurobindo's Ashram is a divine place and if a person comes there and takes up its work, it is the divine force that leads him to take it up and if he does it in the spirit of consecration to the Mother, he will become the Mother's instrument. The very atmosphere of the Ashram will induce him to take up this attitude. Is my faith true?

There may be a power in the atmosphere of the Ashram and there is, but the internal consent of the individual is also necessary.

*

When X came today to join in our work, Y told him jokingly: "Why have you come to this work? It is very difficult. It is better to leave it." Though he was saying this in a humorous way, is it not likely that this sort of talk can do harm to others?

Yes. There is no use in it and it can do harm.

*

Is work indispensable for growing into the spiritual consciousness and realising the Supramental Truth?

The growth out of the ordinary mind into the spiritual consciousness can be effected either by meditation, dedicated work or Bhakti for the Divine. In our Yoga, which seeks not only a static peace or absorption but a dynamic spiritual action, work is indispensable. As for the Supramental Truth, that is a different matter; it depends only on the descent of the Divine and the action of the Supreme Force and is not bound by any method or rule.

*

Is it possible for sadhaks to realise the Supermind through work?

If they have the right consciousness.

*

The Mother has written: "The illusion of action is one of the greatest illusions of human nature." What is meant by illusion here?

Illusion means that they think their action is all important and its egoistic objects are the Truth that must be followed.

*

I have noticed that when I am alone and not doing any work I am full of peace and aspiration but when I come out in the field of work and enter in contact with others, lots of difficulties arise and my peace and aspiration are lost. What is the reason for this?

It is the difficulty of being calm and surrendered in action and movement; when there is no action and one is simply sitting still, it is easy to be quiet.

*

Some people say that a person without literary or artistic capacity cannot progress in sadhana and cannot be an instrument for Divine work. Is this true?

All this is rubbish. Some of those who are progressing most, cannot write well and know no art.

11. *Transformation*

What are the chief obstacles that stand in the way of transformation?

There are only three fundamental obstacles that can stand in the way:
(1) Absence of faith or insufficient faith.
(2) Egoism — the mind clinging to its own ideas, the vital preferring its own desires to a true surrender, the physical adhering to its own habits.
(3) Some inertia or fundamental resistance in the consciousness, not willing to change because it is too much of an effort or because it does not want to believe in its capacity or the power of the Divine — or for some other more subconscient reason. You have to see for yourself which of these it is.

*

What is meant by "the physical adhering to its own habits" in the above answer?

For instance, the body clinging to its own preferences about food or preferring its own habit and convenience to the proper discharge of the work — these are instances of the physical habit.

*

What is "the other subconscient reason" which you mention as a chief obstacle to transformation?

That I cannot say here — it takes a hundred different forms.

*

How to remove "inertia" and "fundamental resistance in the consciousness" which stand in the way of transformation?

There is only one rule for all these things — to look at oneself closely so as to detect these things always when they show themselves, to reject them always and persistently when seen, to aspire always for their removal, to call always the Force of the Mother to help to remove them. But the most entirely effective thing is if you can feel the Force of the Mother working in you and support its action always.

*

What is meant by supporting the action of the Mother's Force which you say is the most effective way of removing inertia or other resistance in the consciousness?

To support its action means that one must recognise the Mother's Force when it acts and distinguish it from other egoistic or ignorant forces and give assent to the one and refuse the others. It is again a general rule — its application each sadhak has to see for himself.

*

How to distinguish the Mother's Force from other egoistic or ignorant forces?

One has only to be perfectly sincere, not to justify one's own desires and faults by the mind's reasonings, to look impartially and quietly at oneself and one's movements and to call on the Mother's Light — then gradually one will begin to discern everything in that light. Even if it cannot be done perfectly at once, the judgment and feeling will get clearer and surer and a right consciousness of these things will be established.

*

If a sadhak cannot fully discriminate between the Mother's Force and the egoistic and ignorant forces and cannot reject them, what will be his condition?

All these questions are met by my answer. One cannot be perfect in discrimination at once or in rejection either. The one indispensable thing is to go on trying sincerely till there comes the full success. So long as there is complete sincerity, the Divine Grace will be there and assist at every moment on the way.

*

You wrote that egoism is one of the chief obstacles in sadhana and described it as "the mind clinging to its own ideas, the vital preferring its own desires to true surrender, the physical adhering to its own habits". What is meant by "true surrender" and when does a sadhak realise it fully?

When he is able to get rid of these things — accept the Knowledge from above in place of his own ideas, the will of the Divine in place of his own desires, the movements of the Truth in place of his physical habits — and as a result is able to live wholly for the Divine.

❧

How can I know what is the Mother's Will? If in doing something I get a feeling of inconvenience does it mean that it is against her Will?

How can your convenience or inconvenience be the indication of the Mother's Will? You have to develop the psychic feeling which distinguishes the truth from the falsehood, the divine from the undivine.

❧

When does transformation begin in a sadhak?

There is no fixed "when".

❧

How can a sadhak know that transformation is going on in him?

If it is happening he will feel it. There is no question of how.

❧

When the nature is purified, is it an indication of transformation?

Transformation is made possible by purification.

*

What is the real meaning of purification?

Purification from desire, ego, falsehood and ignorance.

*

Is it possible to have a partial realisation of the highest Truth without complete purification?

Yes.

*

In what way is it possible?

By openness to the Divine.

*

Is it true that a sadhak will be able to receive the Divine Grace and Truth in proportion to his progress in opening to the Divine and transforming himself?

The more he progresses, the greater the force of the Truth upon him — the more he is transformed, the more he will be able to feel the Divine influence.

*

If a sadhak gets rid of his lower nature, will he realise complete transformation?

If he gets rid of the lower nature, that would mean getting rid of the Ignorance (ego, desire, etc.); so it would necessarily be a complete transformation.

✳

How can one become conscious of the defects of one's nature which remain hidden and become an obstacle to transformation? How can one offer these defects to the Divine for transformation?

One has to be vigilant and watch and also to call down the Mother's Light so that it will show whatever in one is hidden from the mind.

You have only to be perfectly sincere and aspire for purification and reject whatever is wrong in you. The Divine Force will then act and do the rest. That is the simple and true way.

✳

When a sadhak turns his lower nature to the Mother by discrimination, is it called transformation?

No, certainly not. It is only a condition for transformation.

✳

If a sadhak through lack of sufficient discrimination

cannot wholly turn his nature to the Mother, does it become very difficult for the Mother's Force to transform him?

If his discrimination is constant and true and his turning complete, transformation can proceed very rapidly.

※

Is it not possible that a sadhak's nature can be turned to the Mother and transformed by Her Grace without any personal effort on his part?

If there is no personal effort, if the sadhak is too indolent and Tamasic to try, why should the Grace act?

※

Will a sadhak who is only partially transformed not be able to reach the highest Truth?

It is likely.

※

Is it true that transformation is not possible without getting spiritual experiences?

Some change may come — not the transformation of the whole being. How can that happen without any spiritual experiences?

※

When a sadhak gets dreams signifying some spiritual truth, does it not indicate that his nature is getting transformed?

Not necessarily. It shows that he has more consciousness than ordinary people, but dreams do not transform the nature.

12. *Difficulties and Progress*

How long the difficulties and obstacles remain in sadhana?

It depends on the sadhaks.

*

In what sense does it depend on them? Does it mean that the difficulty remains so long as they wish to keep it?

Yes, or so long as something in them gives cause for the difficulties.

*

How is it that the more sincerely we try to face and overcome the difficulties of our nature the more they tend to increase?

It is the opposing or adverse forces that attack because they are afraid of their control over men being taken from them by the success of the sadhana.

*

Whenever I find myself inwardly in a good condition and make a sincere effort to progress I find that the difficulties tend to increase. Why does it happen like this?

It is not you alone who feel that; everybody has that experience.

*

Does this prove that I am incapable of doing Yoga?

In that case it would prove that everybody is incapable — for everybody has the same experience.

*

If a sadhak finds it difficult to make any progress in his sadhana and is constantly faced with difficulties, how will he be able to stay in the Ashram?

I don't understand the question. Those who want to stay and are sincere in the sadhana, can always stay whatever the difficulties.

*

Is it a fact that the sadhaks, so long as they do not overcome the defects of their nature, have to undergo various tests imposed by the Divine?

It is not a test, it is only the natural law that they have to overcome these things before they can realise the aim of Yoga.

*

Is it true that the hostile forces attack and create disturbances in sadhana in order to test the strength of the sadhaks?

The hostile forces make it their function to attack and disturb the sadhaks, but if there were no wrong movement and no imperfection and weakness, they would not be disturbed.

*

How can I know whether I am progressing in sadhana and the transformation of my being by the Mother's Force and Grace?

If it is being done, you will be conscious of it.

*

Some sadhaks in the Ashram say that they do not know if they are making any progress at all because they do not get any feeling indicating progress. What is the reason for this?

It simply shows that they are unconscious.

*

But can it be said that they are really progressing even though they are not feeling any indications of it?

One may have experiences without fully understanding them; but if they feel nothing, then they cannot be said to be progressing.

*

When a sadhak begins to get experiences, does it mean that he is progressing?

It shows that he is progressing.

✳

If a sadhak thinks constantly about his weaknesses and remains unhappy, is it a hindrance in his progress?

Yes. He has to think more of the Divine and less of himself.

✳

Nowadays all kinds of memories of my past life are pressing upon my mind. What is the reason?

They must be coming up from the subconscient in order to be got rid of.

✳

What is the way to get rid of the pressure of these memories?

Clear them out as they come and let nothing in the being accept or interest itself in them any more.

✳

Most of the difficulties and depressions in my sadhana come from the fact that I have a narrow and undeveloped mind. What is the best thing to do to remove this defect?

It is through the psychic that the Yoga develops; the mind is not the chief thing.

✳

Is it not a fact that difficulties and depressions come because of the narrow and undeveloped mind?

More through the vital's dissatisfaction or the physical consciousness and its ignorance and *tamas*.

*

What is the swiftest and most effective way to remove "tamas" or inertia from all the parts of the system?

To call down the Divine Force to act there.

*

Why do I feel my body so inert and dull?

It depends on whether it is in tune with the vital or not. The nature of the body is *tāmasic* — it is the vital which makes it move and uses it as an instrument. If the vital is enlightened then the Divine Force can act throughout in the body.

*

When can the vital be said to be enlightened?

The vital must not only reject all lower movements, but open and receive the light from above so that it may receive and know the Divine Will and its impulsion — it can then be called enlightened.

*

In "Conversations", the Mother says: "The true vital movement is the most beautiful and magnificent of movements." What is this true vital movement?

A movement of the vital in its original divine nature, not full of egoism and selfish passion and desire as it is usually in man.

*

How can I get rid of the difficulties that arise in action and in contact with others?

By rejecting ego and desire and living and working for the Divine alone.

*

When a sadhak is trying to rise to the higher consciousness, how can he prevent the influences of his surroundings from pulling him down?

By indifference to the surroundings and concentration on what is above.

*

Do our thoughts (good or bad) about others affect them in any way?

Yes, there is an influence.

*

Is it possible that the desires, doubts, etc. of one person can pass on to another?

Anything can pass from one to another. It is happening all the time throughout the world.

*

How can one know that the desire or doubt he is having has come from another person?

You have to become conscious.

*

Is it not very harmful to observe the faults of others and criticise them? Does not this habit become a great obstacle in the progress of sadhana?

Yes, all that is true. The lower vital takes a mean and petty pleasure in picking out the faults of others and thereby one hampers both one's own progress and that of the subject of the criticism.

*

Is gossiping an obstacle in sadhana?

It can be and very often is. A gossiping spirit is always an obstacle.

*

Is it true that if a sadhak does anything wrong in-

wardly or outwardly, others in the Ashram have to suffer for it?

It creates a wrong influence in the atmosphere of the Ashram and opens the gates to the hostile Powers.

*

Is it true that when the sadhaks feel uneasiness or disturbance, it is due to their having acted contrary to the Divine's Will?

It comes from that or it comes from imperfections in their nature.

*

When the sadhaks have overcome all the difficulties and obstacles, why do they not go away from the world also for ever?

Why should they? If the sadhaks really overcome all the difficulties, then the higher consciousness gets partly established on the earth — but what of the rest of the world and their imperfect evolution?

*

How can a sadhak remain free from illness?

It is only by the conquest of the material nature that illness can cease altogether to come.

*

If a sadhak gets illnesses for one reason or another, how can he throw them away swiftly?

Most of them can be got rid of almost at once by faith and calling in the Force. Those that are chronic are more difficult but they too can be got rid of by the same means if persistently used.

*

When a sadhak gets an illness, can he make use of physical means like medicines to get over it?

Physical means can be used whenever necessary; but behind the physical means there must be the Divine Force. The physical means are to be used with discrimination and in case of necessity.

*

Is it true that illnesses can come to a sadhak because of want of faith in the Divine?

They come from various causes — what you speak of is a condition that helps them to come and stands in the way of cure.

13. *Sex — Food — Sleep*

Is it true that sexual desire is the greatest obstacle in Yoga?

One of the greatest, at least.

*

Does sexual desire increase by taking more food and decrease by taking less?

It is rather certain kinds of food that are supposed to increase it — e.g., meat, onions, chillies, etc.

*

Are greed, anger, jealousy etc., the companions of sexual desire?

They usually go with sexual desire, though not always.

*

The Mother has said "the strength of such impulses as those of the sex lies usually in the fact that the people take too much notice of them". What is meant by a person taking too much notice of these impulses?

If he is always thinking of them and struggling with them, that is taking too much notice.

*

What should he do to avoid taking too much notice?

He has to detach himself from them, think less of sex and more of the Divine.

*

The Mother has also said in regard to sexual thoughts that it is wrong to "endeavour to control them by coercion, hold them within and sit upon them". How does a person hold these thoughts within and sit upon them?

The words convey their own explanation. If you remain full of sexual thoughts and try to prevent them from manifesting in some kind of action, that is holding them within and sitting on them. It is the same with anger or any other passion. They have to be thrown away, not kept in you.

*

You have said that control of a wrong movement merely suppresses it and that to remove it completely it has to be rejected. What is the utility then of controlling movements of sex, anger, fear, etc.

If your rejection is not successful, you have to control. The control at least prevents you from being the slave of your vital impulses. Once you have the control, it is easier to reject successfully. Absence of control does not bring successful rejection.

*

What is the process of turning the sexual energy into 'ojas'?

If it is to be done by a process, it will have to be by Tapasya (self-control of mind, speech, act) and a drawing upward of the seminal energy through the will. But it can be better done by the descent of the Force and its working on the sex-centre and consequent transformation, as with all other things in this Yoga.

*

Is fasting a help in our sadhana?

This sadhana is not helped by fasting.

*

Is taking very little food helpful in controlling the senses?

No, it simply exasperates them — to take a moderate amount is best. People who fast easily get exalted and may lose their balance.

*

If one takes only vegetarian food, does it help in controlling the senses?

It avoids some of the difficulties which the meat-eaters have, but it is not sufficient by itself.

*

Is sleep necessary for a sadhak who has reached the higher consciousness?

So long as one has a body that is not altogether transformed in all its functionings, sleep is necessary.

*

Why are the mind and vital so active at night?
How could one control their activity at night?

It is their function. So long as one is not perfectly conscious in sleep, they will act.

*

In the first and middle part of my sleep there is a great mental and vital activity but in the last part this activity subsides and I get various kinds of symbolic dreams and intimations of higher knowledge. What is the reason for this?

In sleep one very commonly passes from consciousness to deeper consciousness in a long succession until one reaches the psychic and rests there or else from higher to higher consciousness until one reaches rest in some silence and peace. The few minutes one passes in this rest are the real sleep which restores, — if one does not get it, there is only a half rest. It is when you come near to either of these domains of rest that you begin to see these higher kinds of dreams.

*

What is the way to pass into the psychic or the higher consciousness in sleep and rest there?

It is done unconsciously as it is. If one wants to do it consciously and regulate it, one has first to become conscious in sleep.

*

How to make a heavy subconscient sleep light?

By calling in more consciousness.

*

I have noticed that even half an hour's sleep during day-time refreshes me more that five or six hours' sleep at night. What is the reason for this?

It must be because it is a different kind of sleep in the day-time, less heavy, with less time spent in the subconscient.

*

Some people say that they have dreamless sleep for the whole night. Is this possible?

They simply mean that when they come back, they are not conscious of having dreamed. In the sleep the consciousness goes into other planes and has experiences there and when these are translated perfectly or imperfectly by the physical mind, they are called dreams. All the time of sleep such dreams take place, but sometimes one remembers and at other times does not at all remember. Sometimes also one goes low down into the subconscient and the dreams are there, but so deep down that when one comes out there is not even the consciousness that one had dreamed.

*

Have dreams any significance? Is there any meaning in the dreams of the subconscient?

A dream, when it is not from the subconscient, is either symbolic or else an experience of some supraphysical plane or a formation therein by some mental or vital or other force or in rare cases an indication of some event actual or probable in the past, present or future. A dream from the subconscious plane has no meaning; it is simply a *kichadi* of impressions and memories left in the subconscient from the past.

*

In dream I saw some people climbing up a mountain with great difficulty. I was also climbing with them. After a time I got tired, so I gave up climbing and began to think what was to be done. Then I felt that a force lifted me up lightly and carried me to the top of the mountain. On reaching the top, I saw that there were many beautiful houses of different colours and lights. Then I woke up. What does this dream signify?

It is a symbol of the two methods — one of self-effort, the other of the action of the Mother's Force carrying the sadhak.

*

During sleep I often get bad dreams of the vital plane. How to prevent this?

You can do it by having a will in the waking state against these things coming in the dream, before you go to sleep for instance. It will not succeed at once but it will in the end. Or else you must aspire to grow more conscious in sleep.

*

Sometimes when I have an attack in dream, I can get rid of it by repeating the Mother's name. Does this mean that even the Mother's name has power in it?

Yes, certainly, there is always a power in the Name.

14. *Some Explanations*

Are not religious practices like doing japa, reading holy scriptures, doing puja, etc. signs of aspiration for the Divine life? Are they not a help for reaching the highest Truth?

It depends on the spirit in which they are done. A man can do all these things and yet remain an unspiritual man or even an Asura.

*

Is there any spiritual value in going for pilgrimage to holy places and worshipping many gods and goddesses? Does it help in realising the Divine Truth?

It has nothing to do with the Truth; it is a religious exercise for the ordinary consciousness.

*

What is the spiritual utility of 'saṁkirtan' which is common amongst Vaishnavas?

It has a power of raising devotion, especially in the vital parts.

*

I have read in some religious books that if one mem-

ber of a family has a spiritual realisation, all the other members get Mukti by his influence. How far is this true?

It is not true. Each has his own destiny and his entering into a particular family in one life is only an incident.

*

Ramakrishna used to say that if a person remembers God and utters His name before another person even for a while in any way, it will bear fruit one day and bring about a spiritual change in that person. Can it happen like this?

It can no more be done in that way than you can change a mouse into a lion by saying to it "lion, lion".

*

Is there any possibility of fully turning towards God for people who remain wholly engrossed in worldly life and remember God only in times of difficulty and calamity?

There is a future possibility for every one, even for the atheist or the one who never thinks of God.

*

If even the atheist or one who never thinks of God has a future possibility of fully turning to God, then why should anyone enter the spiritual life and face its difficulties?

The future possibility may only realise after ten thousand years and even then it can only come by practising Yoga.

*

Ordinary people call for the action of the Divine Grace in times of calamity but afterwards forget the Divine. Does the Grace act in the life of people only in this way?

It is only with the ordinary people that it is like that, not with those who seek after the Divine. The special Grace of the Divine is for the seekers of the Divine — for the others it is a Cosmic Will acting through their Karma.

*

Is there any difference between the Divine Will and the Divine Grace? Are they not the same?

The Divine Will works on all things — it may work out anything whatever. The Divine Grace comes in to help and save.

*

Can it be said that a sadhak who in his present life could not fully open himself to the Divine, will in his next birth again take up the Yogic life and continue his sadhana?

Yes, it is fairly certain that he will, unless he has to exhaust first the adverse elements that come in his way before he starts again.

*

Can it be said that those who in their present life follow the worldly pursuits with only a partial turning to the Divine, will in their next life take wholly to spiritual life?

There is no rigid rule for that — they will follow their evolution according to what they have been, are and are aspiring to be.

*

There is a belief that if a person, who never thought of God during his whole life, were only to utter His name or to remember Him at the time of his last breath on his death-bed, he will get mukti in his next life. Is there any truth in this belief?

No — that is all superstition. If mukti were so easy, everybody could do what he liked all his life and simply by the trick of remembering "God" at the end, reach the supreme state. It is an idiotic idea.

*

The Puranas speak of many higher worlds or 'lokas'. Do people after death rise to these 'lokas' and live there?

They only pass through certain, not through all.

*

People believe that a person who leads a good life or a religious life goes to Heaven after death. Is this true?

He has some happy state for a time after death, that is all.

*

The Puranas also say that in the next world there are thousands of Hells and that people who do evil actions in this life have to go and live there after their death. Is this true?

That is a superstition. People after death pass through certain vital and mental worlds or through certain psychological states which are the results of their nature and action in life; afterwards they go to the psychic world and return to earth at a later time.

*

Sometimes in dream I meet and talk to my relatives who died long ago. Why does this happen?

They keep in the vital world the ideas and characteristics of the physical life. It is in the vital that you meet them.

*

Is it possible for a dead relative of a sadhak to come in his way and disturb his sadhana?

Only if the sadhak allows it.

*

Has Astrology no place in Yoga?

Astrology is an occult science — it is not a part of the Yoga except as anything can be made a part of the Yoga — if done in the right spirit.

*

Can one get any help for spiritual life from Astrology?

No.

*

What should be one's attitude towards Astrology?

As any other art or science.

*

What is the place of occult power in Yoga?

To know and use the subtle forces of the supraphysical planes is part of the Yoga.

*

What is the meaning of occult endeavour and power?

It depends on the context. Usually it would mean power to use the secret forces of Nature and an endeavour by means of these forces. But 'occult' may mean something else in another context.

*

Has every Yogi to pass through occult endeavour?

No, everyone has not the capacity. Those who do not have it, must wait till it is given to them.

*

Is Divine Shakti the same as Yogic Shakti — the powers which Yogis develop by tapasya?

That kind of Yogic Shakti is not the same as the Divine Shakti. Even the Asura and the Rakshasa have powers. The real Yoga Shakti is that which comes from contact or union with the Divine consciousness and its workings.

*

Do miracles happen in a sadhak's life?

What do you mean by a miracle? What people call miracle is only something done in a striking way by a process unknown to them which their minds cannot follow.

*

Does Yogic siddhi mean the power to do something miraculously? Is there anything wrong in using such a power if a sadhak has realised it?

I have explained that there is no such thing as a miracle. If a higher consciousness opens a higher power in him, the sadhak has to use it as part of the new consciousness but in the right way without egoism, selfishness, vanity or pride.